TAKE A LESSON
IN POETRY

John King

foulsham  educational

LONDON • NEW YORK • TORONTO • SYDNEY

TAKE A LESSON
IN POETRY

foulsham

The Publishing House, Bennetts Close,
Cippenham, Slough, Berks SL1 5AP England

ISBN 0-572-02276-X

MV 18/2/04

Printed in Great Britain

CONTENTS

FOREWORD

Poetry can communicate from one mind to another, from one generation to another, more effectively than any other means. I wrote this book to help my students write their own poems with greater confidence and with better understanding of basic poetic conventions. If you are a teacher, use it as I have done – to make writing poems fun, a pleasurable activity, a reward in itself. If you are a student, use it to help you write, but also to help you read – there is a whole lifetime's treasure of good poetry waiting to be found, once you know how to start looking.

Most importantly of all, this is a *doing* book, not just a reading book. It's a workshop, where you can practise hammering words into ideas to hold them together, shaping expression to fit experience, knocking out hand-made poems, throwing away the ones you don't like and polishing up the ones you do so you can take them home to show off to your Mum. Put them on the mantlepiece. Send them to your local paper, or a publisher. Put them together with somebody else in a poetry magazine, or send them to someone you love. Bury them in a time capsule. It's up to you!

Some technical words are used in the text. They are usually printed in bold italics and explained whenever they first occur and the explanations are repeated in a very simple glossary at the back of the book.

My thanks are due to Kath Williams of Pool School and Heather Hugh of Redruth School for their good-humoured encouragement and advice.

POETRY IN THE NATIONAL CURRICULUM

The National Curriculum for English is concerned, above all, to develop in pupils the skills of effective communication: writing, speaking and literacy, and to encourage them to be responsive to what they read in ways that are knowledgeable and enthusiastic.

John King has written *Take a Lesson in Poetry* with these requirements in mind. Each of the twelve units focuses on the key compositional skills:

- Developing ideas

- Communicating meaning

- Broadening vocabulary

- Developing effective style

- Organising and structuring work

- Creating coherence

John King helps to build a sound knowledge base for pupils to work from, explaining how and why poetry works – in all its variety of form. It is through the medium of poetry that pupils are encouraged to respond to language and ideas in ways which are non-threatening and fun.

The extracts and complete poems that are presented are drawn from a range of oral and literary traditions, and introduce pupils to a variety of styles and language from classic favourites such as Eliot, Joyce and Longfellow to a breadth of modern writers.

Pupils are challenged to extend their own ideas and their emotional understanding of life, and are encouraged to explore these experiences through a range of imaginative and absorbing tasks, some of which lead naturally into the type of research skills that are needed for project work. These tasks include such key skills as:

- Personal response

- Reading and learning by heart

- Exploring other cultures and traditions

- Inferring and deducing

- Working in pairs or groups

- Understanding gist and the details

- Making presentations

Take a Lesson in Poetry really is a workshop and, as the term implies, is actively based. John King provides a wealth of material which supports the aims of the National Curriculum in English by stimulating pupils' imagination and enthusiasm, and by challenging them to respond to the richness of the written word with understanding and enthusiasm.

1
RIDDLE POEMS

Poems are meant to be read more than once. Sometimes you don't even know what a poem is about until you have read it two or three times. There are some poems which don't seem to make much sense for years, until you're old enough to have lived through the kind of events they are describing.

The following poems shouldn't take you years to work out. They are all riddle poems; you have to guess what they are about or what they are describing. The answers are printed at the end of this section, but try to resist the temptation to cheat – it's much more fun trying to work out the answers for yourself. ("Anon", incidentally, stands for anonymous, meaning nobody knows who wrote the poem – some of these riddles were written hundreds of years ago!)

1. I am puff-breasted, proud-crested,
   a head I have, and a high tail,
   eyes and ears and one foot,
   both my sides, a back that's hollow,
   a very stout beak, a steeple neck
   and a home above men.
       Harsh are my sufferings
   when that which makes the forest tremble
   takes and shakes me.
   Here I stand under streaming rain
   and blinding sleet, stoned by hail;
   freezes the frost and falls the snow
   on me stuck-bellied. And I stick it all out
   for I cannot change the chance that made me.

   (Anon)

2. Little Nancy Etticoat,
   In a white petticoat,
   And a red nose;
   The longer she stands,
   The shorter she grows.

   (Anon)

3. In marble halls as white as milk,
   Lined with a skin as soft as silk,
   Within a fountain crystal clear
   A golden apple doth appear.
   No doors are there to this stronghold,
   Yet thieves break in and steal the gold.

   (Anon)

4. There is one that has a head without an eye,
   And there's one that has an eye without a head:
   You may find the answer if you try;
       And when all is said,
   Half the answer hangs upon a thread.

   (Anon)

5. I went to the wood and got it.
   I sat me down and looked for it.
   The more I searched for it, the less I liked it.
   I brought it home, because I couldn't find it.

   (Anon)

6. A bit of jungle in the street
   He goes on velvet toes,
   And slinking through the shadows, stalks
   Imaginary foes.

   (Anon)

7. I bring fresh showers for the thirsting flowers,
       From the seas and the streams;
   I bear light shade for the leaves when laid
       In their noonday dreams.
   From my wings are shaken the dews that waken
       The sweet buds every one,
   When rocked to rest on their mother's breast,
       As she dances about the sun.
   I wield the flail of the flashing hail,
       And whiten the green plains under
   And then again I dissolve it in rain,
       And laugh as I pass in thunder.

   (P.B. Shelley)

The last two "riddles" are complete poems. You might need to use a dictionary to find the meanings of some of the words, but can you guess what each poem is describing? (Two cryptic clues: number 8 is what Lampwick turned into and Pinocchio almost turned into on Pleasure Island, and number 9 comes in all shapes and sizes, even a Daily one!)

8. When fishes flew and forests walked
       And figs grew upon thorn,
   Some moment when the moon was blood
       Then surely I was born.

   With monstrous head and sickening cry
       And ears like errant wings,
   The devil's walking parody
       On all four-footed things.

   The tattered outlaw of the earth,
       Of ancient crooked will;
   Starve, scourge, deride me: I am dumb,
       I keep my secret still.

   Fools! For I also had my hour;
       One far fierce hour and sweet:
   There was a shout about my ears,
       And palms before my feet.

                    (*G.K. Chesterton*)

9. I am silver and exact. I have no preconceptions.
Whatever I see I swallow immediately
Just as it is, unmisted by love or dislike.
I am not cruel, only truthful –
The eye of a little god, four-cornered.
Most of the time I meditate on the opposite wall.
It is pink, with speckles. I have looked at it so long
I think it is a part of my heart. But it flickers.
Faces and darkness separate us over and over.

Now I am a lake. A woman bends over me,
Searching my reaches for what she really is.
Then she turns to those liars, the candles or the moon.
I see her back and reflect it faithfully.
She rewards me with tears and an agitation of hands.
I am important to her. She comes and goes.
Each morning it is her face that replaces the darkness.
In me she has drowned a young girl, and in me an old woman
Rises toward her day after day, like a terrible fish.

(*Sylvia Plath*)

Exercises

1. Using the Library, or English Department books, or your own, find three poems which describe something without actually naming it. Copy the poems out and swap them with a partner, who has to guess what they are describing.

2. Find a book of poems and see if there are any riddle poems among them – read them out to the class.

3. Write three riddle poems of your own, starting "I am . . .". You have to give enough information to make it clear *exactly* what you are (for example, if you just write "I am big and green", you could mean anything from a marrow to a football pitch!) but you have to hide your identity by choosing your words cleverly. Try to find words that can mean different things in different places (for example, "I'm hot and I've got spots" – the Sun). Don't worry about rhyme: just start a new line for each new thought. Read them out for the class to guess.

4. Imagine you're a Martian visiting Earth for the first time. Describe a very familiar Earth object without naming it and as if you didn't have a clue what it might be used for.

Answers to Riddles

1. A weathercock.
2. A candle.
3. An egg.
4. A pin and a needle.
5. A thorn.
6. An alley cat.
7. A cloud.
8. A donkey.
9. A mirror.

2
WORD POWER

It seems pretty daft to say that most (not all!) poems are written with words, but it is worth pointing out how important individual words are in creating poetry.

Words have power. They can please us, move us, soothe us, or offend us (think of some choice swear words or insults, but don't actually say them!) The ancient Celts believed that it was possible actually to kill someone simply by speaking a curse against them, and to this day many people believe that some words have special magic or holy powers. Are there any words which affect you strongly?

Poetry uses powerful words and phrases to convey ideas, moods and emotions. The words may be rare or difficult, but more usually they are ordinary words used in an unusual or striking way. Sometimes the results are very concentrated, and you have to add your own thoughts, ideas and reactions to get the full sense of what the poet is trying to say – like diluting concentrated fruit squash with water so you can drink it. Some words in a poem may work very hard to achieve that concentrated effect.

For example, here is a very short extract from a poem by the Welsh poet Dylan Thomas, in which he describes rising from the grave on the Day of Judgement:

> I shall waken
> To the judge blown bedlam
> Of the uncaged sea bottom
> The cloud climb of the exhaling tomb
> And the bidden dust upsailing
> With his flame in every grain.

On first reading, you probably found that almost impossible to understand, although you'll have formed a vague mental picture of what's being described. It's only when you look more closely at each word and group of words that you can begin to explain how that picture in your mind is created.

For example, the phrase "cloud climb of the exhaling tomb" creates all these images for me: a grave breathing, as if it were itself alive; the grave's breath being its last breath, because it is "exhaling", breathing out to give life to the body it contains; dust rising in clouds, perhaps even exploding upwards; "earth to earth, ashes to ashes, dust to dust", the human body being reduced from flesh to dust, and then blowing away, like sand in a desert; light swirling through the dust; ghosts or spirits rising up in the dust cloud; the spirits taking human shape, as the light swirls through the cloud of dust; the cloud climbing ("climb" because it's living – "rise" wouldn't achieve the same effect) towards heaven.

Those **images**, or pictures in the mind, are made stronger for me by the words "uncaged" in the previous line and "upsailing" in the following line. Perhaps different images will have formed for you, but I hope you can see how a few words can create a very rich, complicated mental picture.

Words can make us smile, blush, or want to punch somebody on the nose. Individual words can create emotional impact just by their meaning, or by how other people have used them and what feelings they have come to be associated with. What *one* word would you most like other people to use to describe you? Handsome? Clever? Kind? And what one word would you *least* like other people to use about you? Fat? Ugly? Greedy?

But words also influence emotion by the sound they make, particularly when they are grouped together in musical patterns. Here is a short extract from a poem called 'Lepanto' by G.K. Chesterton. Which words are meant to influence our emotions, and how are they grouped together by sound?

> Strong gongs groaning as the guns boom far,
> Don John of Austria is going to the war,
> Stiff flags straining in the night-blasts cold
> In the gloom black-purple, in the glint old-gold,
> Torchlight crimson on the copper kettle-drums,
> Then the tuckets, then the trumpets, then the cannon,
>   and he comes.
> Don John laughing in the brave beard curled,
> Spurning of his stirrups like the thrones of all the
>   world,
> Holding his head up for a flag of all the free.
> Love-light of Spain – hurrah!
> Death-light of Africa!
> Don John of Austria
> Is riding to the sea.

Does the poet want us to like Don John, or not? How can you tell?

When you read poems by other people, sometimes the most useful first question you can ask yourself is: what is the writer trying to make me feel about what he or she is describing? Happy? Sad? Angry?

That's also a useful starting point for your own poems: how do you want the reader to react?

Here is a short poem written many years ago (by our friend good old Anon!):

> O the cuckoo she's a pretty bird,
>   She singeth as she flies,
> She bringeth good tidings,
>   She telleth no lies.
>
> She sucketh white flowers
>   For to keep her voice clear,
> And the more she singeth cuckoo
>   The summer draweth near.

It only takes a few small changes to completely alter the purpose of that poem:

> O the cuckoo she's a noisy bird,
>   She cackles as she flies,
> She brings us evil tidings,
>   She tells us only lies.
>
> She sucks brown rotting flowers
>   To keep her voice full strong,
> And while she cackles cuckoo
>   The summer drags along.

Some words have richer and more interesting sounds than others. There is a theory that language itself began because primitive man imitated the sounds of animals and the forest around him, so some words still sound like the things they represent: splash, plop, whizz, fizzle, crackle, and so on. This is called **onomatopoeia**.

If words make similar sounds to each other, usually by beginning with the same letter (like "cloud" and "climb"), that too produces a musical effect, which is called **alliteration**.

We'll look more closely at the music made by words in later chapters.

Here is a poem with some words missing. Bearing in mind the need to choose words for their meaning, for the emotions they create, and for the sound they make, what words would you put in the blank spaces? I have put the original words at the end of this section, although your suggestions may be just as good, if not better than the originals.

The Happiest Places

The happiest places I have ever known
Have been the wildest ones,
Grey nettles and   (a)   stones,
And overhead a   (b)   roof of green.
Down some   (c)   bank of chalk, or gravel-pit,
No use for man nor beast,
Forgotten stuff and mast,
Where   (d)   hang webs and cuckoo-spit.

The sun smells   (e)   on elder or on fern,
And wild things   (f)   there
Wings busy in the air,
While secretly the   (g)   children learn
How to find eggs, or wear their trousers through,
And watch the white clouds grow
Like   (h)   that feed on blue,
And how to fall and fight and know.

(David Holbrook)

Exercises

1. Complete this poem twice by filling in the blanks: first with words which make the house seem a horrible, evil place, then secondly, with words which make the house seem very friendly, warm and attractive.

> I climbed the . . . . . stairway,
> Along the . . . . . hall,
> And gazed up at the . . . . .
> Hanging on the wall.
>
> The windows, ... and . . . . .,
> Seemed . . . . . to me;
> They . . . . . out at a . . . . . view
> Across the . . . . . lea.
>
> My heart felt . . . . . and . . . . .
> My thoughts with . . . . . ran wild,
> Returning to that . . . . . house
> I first knew as a child.

2. Find a poem in the Library or in poetry books; copy it out and explain how some of the words or phrases create pictures in your mind.
3. Make two lists of words, the first of words which you find pleasant and attractive, the second of words which you find ugly or harsh sounding; use your lists to create two poems.

Missing Words from 'The Happiest Places'

(a) grey
(b) tangled
(c) rough
(d) undisturbed
(e) strong
(f) scuttle
(g) hidden
(h) sheep

3
SOUND AND SHAPE

Words are the building bricks with which poems are made; the more you know, the more you can use. Suppose, for example, you wanted to describe a cat asleep in a poem. You could say, "The cat sleeps." But, as long as you knew the words, you could also say "The cat naps . . . dozes . . . drowzes . . . lounges . . . nods . . . snores . . . snoozes . . .", and so on. A useful place to find words grouped together by meaning like this is in a book called a *thesaurus*.

Words are also grouped together by sound. We've already met onomatopoeia, where words sound like the thing they are describing, for example, "splash", "swish", "zip", "crunch", "dollop". We've also met alliteration, where words begin with or contain the same sounds to create a musical effect, for example, "brave, bright swords stained in bloody battle" or "the little petals fall in leaflike patterns".

The most familiar grouping of words in poetry is by *rhyme*, which we'll look at in more detail in Chapter 6.

Most people can recognise a poem without even reading it, because it seems that poems are usually set out in regular short lines, making a distinctive shape on the page. We can imitate the shape of a poem without even using words at all. For example, here is a poem by Christian Morgenstern called "Night Song of the Fish", which you could "read" aloud simply by making up sounds for each of the symbols and then saying them – try to sound as fishy as you can!

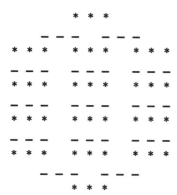

Here is another very strange looking poem. Try saying it out loud, either on your own, with a partner, or in small groups (and remember to take notice of the punctuation!). When you've performed the poem, see if you can think of a title for it. (I've put the actual title and the name of the poet who wrote it at the end of this section, but don't cheat!)

Sssnnwhoffffl?
Hnwhoffl hhnnwfl hnfl hfl?
Gdroblboblhobngbl gbl gl g g g g gl bgl.
Drublhaflablhaflubhafgabhaflhafl fl fl –
gm grawwwww grf grawf awfgm graw gm.
Hovoplodok – doplodovok – plovodokot – doplodokosh?
Splgraw fok fok splgrafhatchgrabrlgabr I fok splfok!
Zgra kra gka fok!
Grof grawff gahf?
Gombl mbl bl –
blm plm,
blm plm,
blm plm,
blp.

You can have a lot of fun experimenting with sounds and shapes in poems. Sometimes poems are written so that the lines form the shape of what they are describing. I'm sure you can work out the one-word title of this poem by Ian Hamilton Finlay without too much difficulty:

```
a       a       a       a       a
    c       c       c       c
r       r       r       r       r
    o       o       o       o
b       b       b       b       b
    a       a       a       a
t       t       t       t       t
    s       s       s       s
t       t       t       t       t
    a       a       a       a
b       b       b       b       b
    o       o       o       o
r       r       r       r       r
    c       c       c       c
a       a       a       a       a
```

(If you need a clue, "circus" should help you.)

As long ago as the seventeenth century, a poet called George Herbert wrote a "shape-poem" called 'Easter Wings'. It was originally printed vertically so that the reader could see the shape of the wings of two angels standing side by side – if you turn the book sideways, you'll get the same effect:

Lord, who createdst man in wealth and store,
Though foolishly he lost the same,
Decaying more and more,
Till he became
Most poore:
With thee
O let me rise
As larks, harmoniously,
And sing this day thy victories:
Then shall the fall further the flight in me.

My tender age in sorrow did beginne:
And still with sicknesses and shame
Thou didst so punish sinne,
That I became
Most thinne.
With thee
Let me combine
And feel this day thy victorie:
For, if I imp my wing on thine,
Affliction shall advance the flight in me.

Sometimes the sounds of a poem are deliberately chosen to be difficult to say, to make your tickly tongue twist trickily. Try these for size:

> If Peter Piper picked a peck
> of pickled peppers,
> where's the peck of pickled peppers
> Peter Piper picked?

> If he could sell her salt,
> I could sell her a salt-cellar
> for salt for her celery.

> Red leather, yellow lorry,
> Yellow leather, red lorry.

> She said she should show
> a soldier her shoulder.

> Left, right, light, rift,
> Fight, let, rife, lift.

But the real purpose in choosing interesting sounding words and putting them into a pleasing shape is to create a satisfying pattern, like good music. The following verses are from a long poem by Alfred Lord Tennyson called 'In Memoriam', written after his close friend had died. Say the poem aloud and notice how the choice of words, the shape of the poem, and the onomatopoeia and alliteration combine to create a very musical effect.

> Calm is the morn without a sound,
>   Calm as to suit a calmer grief,
>   And only thro' the faded leaf
> The chestnut pattering to the ground;

> Calm and deep peace on this high wold,
>   And on these dews that drench the furze,
>   And all the silvery gossamers
> That twinkle into green and gold:

> Calm and still light on yon great plain
>   That sweeps with all its autumn bowers,
>   And crowded farms and lessening towers,
> To mingle with the bounding main:

Calm and deep peace in this wide air,
    These leaves that redden to the fall;
    And in my heart, if calm at all,
If any calm, a calm despair:

Calm on the seas, and silver sleep
    And waves that sway themselves in rest,
    And dead calm in that noble breast
Which heaves but with the heaving deep.

Exercises

1. On your own, or with a partner, write some lists of words grouped together by meaning, using a thesaurus to help you. For example, you could put together a list of words describing the movement of water ("flow", "ripple", "cascade", "flood", etc.) or the movement of an animal – or anything you like. Then try to weave your words into a poem.

2. To practise alliteration, write the longest sentence you can think of in which every word in the sentence (and it must be *every* word) begins with the same letter. Score one point for every word and see who can score the highest. Here's a twelve-pointer: "Bring Brian's boots back by bus, Benjamin, but be back before breakfast."

3. Write some tongue-twisters of your own and get a partner to try saying them out loud.

4. Write a poem like the 'Sssnnnwhoffffl?' poem, just using letters for sounds. Don't forget the punctuation!

5. Write a poem like 'Acrobats' or 'Eastern Wings', in which some words or letters are in unusual positions or making a pattern which suggests what they are describing.

6. Using poetry books from the Library or elsewhere, find any poem which you think creates a pleasing or interesting musical effect, then read it (or sing/act/perform it) for the rest of the class.

"Sssnnwhoffffl?"

The actual title of the "Sssnnwhoffffl?" poem is 'The Loch Ness Monster's Song' by Edwin Morgan.

4

RHYTHM 1

All language has rhythm. Words are spoken, sometimes slowly, sometimes quickly, but always in a sequence which is bound to produce a rhythm, no matter how simple.

The simplest rhythmical sequence would be one in which each word had only one beat or pulse to it, like this:

One day I went home and there was a note from my Mum on the door which said my tea was in the bin. "What a shame," I thought.

You could read those sentences like a Dalek, giving each word exactly the same pitch, length and volume, but it would be very unnatural – indeed, inhuman – to speak that way normally. In practice, you would tend to speak some of the words more loudly and with greater emphasis than others – "day", "home", "note", "Mum", and so on.

Try saying the two sentences above with:
(a) no emphasis at all, like a Dalek or robot;
(b) normal emphasis and rhythm;
(c) exaggerated or unusual emphasis, i.e. in the "wrong" places.

What do you notice about the sentences when you say them differently? Do they change in meaning slightly? Do they produce a different emotional effect in the audience?

The word used to describe the beat, pulse or sound unit in words is *syllable*. In the example sentences above, all the words are *monosyllables*; in other words, each word has only one syllable.

It makes no difference how many letters there are in the word; "a" has one letter, "straight" has eight letters, but they both have only one rhythmic beat, so they are both monosyllables. Here are some more one-syllable words:

dog   cat   no   I   thin   cheese   frog   black   fought   greased

Now here is a list of words, each of which has two syllables:

lemon	hopeless	reward	groggy	Simon	polecat
	intense	apple	regret	greasy	

You may have noticed that a two-syllable word may be shorter than a one-syllable word. For example, "greasy" (two syllables) has fewer letters than "greased" (one syllable).

You may also have noticed that in a two-syllable word, one of the syllables naturally tends to be pronounced with greater emphasis than the other. For example, "le–" in "lemon" is pronounced with greater emphasis than "–mon". We use the words *stress* or **accent** to describe this greater emphasis. We can even mark the stressed syllable with an accent mark, like this:

$$\acute{\text{le}} \text{ mon} \qquad \acute{\text{Si}} \text{ mon} \qquad \acute{\text{hope}} \text{ less}$$

There are some words in the list above which have a different rhythmic pattern. The stress in these words is on the second syllable rather than the first. One of them is:

$$\text{re}\acute{\text{ward}}$$

Can you say which other two words in the list are also stressed on the second syllable?

Some words actually change their meaning according to how they are stressed. The word written "refuse", for example, can be pronounced in two different ways:

$$\acute{\text{re}}\text{fuse} \qquad \text{re}\acute{\text{fuse}}$$

Which word means "rubbish" and which word means "say no"?

Stress patterns in words can also change over time. The word written "defence" in standard English is normally pronounced:

$$\text{de}\acute{\text{fence}}$$

But the popularity of American football on television has introduced many of its fans to the pronunciation:

$$\acute{\text{de}}\text{fence}$$

Perhaps that pronunciation will eventually become the accepted form in standard English.

Try counting the number of syllables in the following words. You should see a very simple pattern emerging:

dog   cherry   elephant   loganberry   unfortunately
disproportionately   conspiratorially   prestidigitationally

This well known word has thirty-four letters, but how many *syllables* does it contain?

Supercalifragilisticexpialidocious

The pattern of stresses in a series of words produces a rhythm. A **regular** rhythm will repeat the same pattern many times:

Downward through the evening twilight,

In the days that are forgotten,

In the unremembered ages,
From the full moon fell Nokomis,

Fell the beautiful Nokomis,

She a wife, but not a mother.

(*H.W. Longfellow: 'The Song of Hiawatha'*)

Whether it's in prose or in poetry, a regular rhythm produces a musical effect. See if you can make up a string of sentences with a strictly regular rhythmical pattern. Here's an example for you. Try saying it aloud, emphasising the stressed syllables (/) and putting less emphasis on the unstressed syllables (ˇ). You should hear a very regular ONE-two-three-four rhythm:

If you're shopping on a Tuesday and you're swimming on a

Sunday, then the only way to meet you is by going to the

station. I can make a reservation if you just give me the

money, and I'll tell you when I get there how to percolate

the coffee.

Some poems rhyme, some don't, but all well written poems have a definite rhythm, just like music. It may be a regular rhythm, like this:

> Ann, Ann!
> Come quick as you can!
> There's a fish that talks
> In the frying-pan.
> Out of the fat,
> As clear as glass,
> He put up his mouth
> And moaned 'Alas!'
> Oh, most mournful,
> 'Alas, alack!'
> Then turned to his sizzling,
> And sank him back.

> *(Walter de la Mare)*

Or the rhythm may be **irregular**, like this:

> A snake came to my water-trough
> On a hot, hot day, and I in pyjamas for the heat,
> To drink there.
>
> In the deep, strange-scented shade of the great dark carob-tree
> I came down the steps with my pitcher
> And must wait, must stand and wait, for there he was at the trough
>   before me.

> *(D.H. Lawrence: 'Snake')*

Can you hear how in the second poem the long last line helps to describe the feeling of waiting a long time?

Rhythm makes language easier to control. If you were to try saying the alphabet backwards, you would probably find it quite difficult to remember; but if you add "and" a few times and set it out in lines to make the rhythm more regular, it becomes much easier:

> Z, Y, X, and W, V,
> U, T, S, and R, Q, P,
> O, N, M, and L, K, J,
> I, H, G,
> F, E, D,
> C, B, A.

We're used to regular rhythmic speech from our earliest childhood games and skipping rhymes:

> Eenie, meenie, mackeracka,
> Hi, di, dominacka,
> Stickeracka, roomeracka,
> Om, pom, push.

Combining regular and irregular rhythms cleverly in writing can produce a very pleasing musical effect. Here, for example, is the very last paragraph of the novel *Moby Dick*; it's a straightforward description of the sea immediately after Captain Ahab's ship has sunk, yet the rhythm of the language creates a powerful emotional atmosphere:

> Now small fowls flew screaming over the yet yawning gulf;
> a sullen white surf beat against its steep sides; then all
> collapsed, and the great shroud of the sea rolled on as it
> rolled five thousand years ago.

> *(Herman Melville: Moby Dick)*

Poetry uses rhythm in exactly the same way to achieve a powerful, musical effect. The following poem doesn't rhyme, but it has a very regular rhythm of four beats to each line. Say the poem aloud, or copy it out with accent marks, to show where the four beats are in each line:

> You remember Davies? He died, you know,
> With his face to the wall, as the manner is
> Of the poor peasant in his stone croft
> On the Welsh hills. I recall the room
> Under the slates, and the smirched snow
> Of the wide bed in which he lay,
> Lonely as an ewe that is sick to lamb
> In the hard weather of mid-March.
> I remember also the trapped wind
> Tearing the curtains, and the wild light's
> Frequent hysteria upon the floor,
> The bare floor without a rug
> Or mat to soften the loud tread
> Of neighbours crossing the uneasy boards
> To peer at Davies with gruff words
> Of meaningless comfort, before they turned
> Heartless away from the stale smell
> Of death in league with those dank walls.

(R.S. Thomas: 'Death of a Peasant')

Exercises

1. Write a poem in which the first line has one syllable, the second two syllables, the third three syllables, and so on, up to say eight or ten syllables per line, then back down again if you wish. Don't worry about rhyme, just concentrate on regular syllables. Here's an example:

> I
> do not
> ever hope
> to be beside
> the sunny seaside
> getting an even tan
> like all the other brownies
> sunning themselves to morning toast.
> When old Mister Sun sees me
> he chucks in more hot rays .
> and my dough-white flesh
> from top to toe
> (unlike bread)
> just goes
> red.

2. Write a few short poems with very regular rhythms. Here are some traditional patterns you might like to follow:

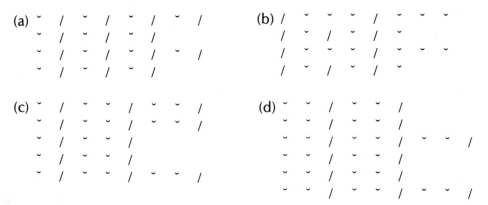

3. Write a poem with four strong beats to each line. Don't use rhyme at all, but concentrate on shaping each line to make a clear, strong rhythmical pattern.

4. Write a poem in which you deliberately contrast long, rhythmically complicated lines with short lines of monosyllables.

5
RHYTHM 2 – SOME PATTERNS

Over the centuries, many different patterns of rhythm have been used in poetry. Many poems were originally written to be sung or chanted, so they have a rhythm as regular as a song; in fact, we still use the same word, **lyrics**, to describe both short poems with regular rhythms and, more recently, the words of songs. In some poems, the rhythm may be irregular, but the number of syllables in each line is fixed.

The kind of poem known as a **haiku**, from its original Japanese name, has a fixed pattern of three lines with five syllables in the first and last lines, and seven syllables in the middle line, although not all modern haiku poems follow this pattern exactly. The stress can fall anywhere. Here's one I wrote:

> The leaping salmon
> Struggled but was sluggish so
> Now he's sliced and tinned.

Although it is fairly easy to write lines which fit the rhythmical pattern, the art of haiku is to paint a detailed picture using words as economically and effectively as possible. Here is another example:

> Bright the full moon shines:
> on the matting of the floor
> shadows of the pines.

(*Translated from the Japanese by H.G. Henderson*)

Have a go at writing some haikus of your own, after reading these two comic examples to remind you of the rhythmic pattern you have to follow:

> cuck oo cuck oo cuck
> oo cuck oo cuck oo cuck oo
> cuck oo cuck oo cuck

(*Roger McGough: 'First Haiku of Spring'*)

Haiku, you ku, he,
She, or it kus, we ku, you
Ku, they ku. Thang ku.

(*Ted Hipple: 'The Traditional Grammarian As Poet'*)

The most common rhythmical unit in English poetry is an unstressed syllable followed by a stressed syllable – dah-DAH dah-DAH dah-DAH, etc. This rhythm is sometimes called ***iambic***.

˘ / ˘ / ˘ / ˘ /
I wander'd lonely as a cloud

˘ / ˘ / ˘ / ˘ /
That floats on high o'er vales and hills,

˘ / ˘ / ˘ / ˘ /
When all at once I saw a crowd,

˘ / ˘ / ˘ / ˘ /
A host of golden daffodils . . .

(*William Wordsworth: 'Daffodils'*)

The iambic rhythm is very common, even in poetry which has no rhyme. Shakespeare and other poets often wrote a form of poetry called ***blank verse***, in which each line was usually ten syllables long, often made up of five repetitions of the iambic pattern. This line pattern is also sometimes referred to as ***iambic pentameter***, meaning iambic five-measure. Here, for example, is a speech from one of Shakespeare's plays in which the King is encouraging his army to fight; see how many lines you can find in it which have the regular iambic pentameter pattern of ˘ / ˘ / ˘ / ˘ / :

This day is call'd the feast of Crispian:
He that outlives this day, and comes safe home,
Will stand a tip-toe when this day is nam'd,
And rouse him at the name of Crispian.
He that shall live this day, and see old age,
Will yearly on the vigil feast his neighbours,
And say 'Tomorrow is Saint Crispian:'
Then will he strip his sleeve and show his scars,
And say, 'These wounds I had on Crispian's day.'
Old men forget: yet all shall be forgot,
But he'll remember with advantages
What feats he did that day.

(*William Shakespeare: 'Henry V' IV, iii*)

Some modern poets deliberately use very simple, everyday speech rhythms; here's an example by William Carlos Williams:

This is Just to Say

I have eaten
the plums
that were in
the icebox

and which
you were probably
saving
for breakfast

Forgive me
they were delicious
so sweet
and so cold

But even everyday speech rhythms vary. For example, it is common in Cornish dialect for words and phrases to be repeated rhythmically, with a rising tone at the end of the sentence:

> 'E dawn knaw nuff to knaw 'e dawn knaw nuffen 'bout nuffen, do 'a, boy?

> 'Ere, boy, dawn knaw naw-one got no dunkey for sale or no, do 'ee or no, boy?

Some dialects and regional accents are well known for their lyrical, rhythmical quality. The Welsh poet Dylan Thomas, for example, in his play '*Under Milk Wood*' describes a character's

> "nicotine eggyellow weeping walrus Victorian moustache worn thick and long in memory of Doctor Crippen".

That long, heavily rhythmic wording is typical of his work – so typical, in fact, that another poet, Robert Graves, accused Dylan Thomas of being "drunk with melody".

Some poems have rhythmic patterns suited to the mood or the movement they are describing. If you read the following poem by Robert Louis Stevenson aloud you should be able to hear the rhythm of a train clackety-clacking along the tracks:

> Faster than fairies, faster than witches,
> Bridges and houses, hedges and ditches;
> And charging along like troops in battle,
> All through the meadows the horses and cattle;
> All of the sights of the hill and the plain
> Fly as thick as driving rain;
> And ever again, in the wink of an eye,
> Painted stations whistle by.
>
> Here is a child who clambers and scrambles,
> All by himself and gathering brambles;
> Here is a tramp who stands and gazes;
> And there is the green for stringing the daisies!
> Here is a cart run away in the road
> Lumping along with man and load;
> And here is a mill, and there is a river:
> Each a glimpse and gone for ever!

Here is another example of a very definite rhythm matching the sound of what is being described:

> I sprang to the stirrup, and Joris, and he;
> I galloped, Dirck galloped, we galloped all three:
> "God speed!" cried the watch, as the gate-bolts undrew;
> "Speed!" echoed the wall to us galloping through;
> Behind shut the postern, the lights sank to rest,
> And into the midnight we galloped abreast . . .

> (Robert Browning: 'How They Brought the Good News from Ghent to Aix')

Some poems have extra lines which are there simply to keep a regular musical rhythm going, even though they don't make any sense themselves – lines like "with a fol-de-rol my Lady-O" or "with a harum-scarum diddle-dum-darum whipsee diddle-dee dandy-O". Here's an example:

> It was a lover and his lass,
>   With a hey, and a ho, and a hey nonino,
> That o'er the green corn-field did pass,
>   In the spring time, the only pretty ring time,
> When birds do sing, hey ding a ding, ding;
> Sweet lovers love the spring . . .

> (William Shakespeare: 'As You Like It', V, iii)

When the Victorian poet Algernon Charles Swinburne published the following lines in his poem 'Atalanta in Calydon', students were so excited and intoxicated by the powerful rhythm of the lines that they chanted them in the streets in thundering voices late at night, much to the annoyance of people trying to get to sleep!:

> When the hounds of spring are on winter's traces,
> The mother of months in meadow or plain
> Fills the shadows and windy places
> With lisp of leaves and ripple of rain;
> And the brown bright nightingale amorous
> Is half assuaged for Itylus,
> For the Thracian ships and the foreign faces,
> The tongueless vigil and all the pain;
> Bind on thy sandals, O thou most fleet,
> Over the splendour and speed of thy feet;
> For the faint east quickens, the wan west shivers,
> Round the feet of the day and the feet of the night.

A complete contrast to that pounding rhythm is this gentle, rocking lullaby by another Victorian poet, Alfred Lord Tennyson:

Sweet and low, sweet and low,
Wind of the western sea,
Low, low, breathe and blow,
Wind of the western sea!
Over the rolling waters go,
Come from the dying moon, and blow,
    Blow him again to me;
While my little one, while my pretty one, sleeps.

Sleep and rest, sleep and rest,
Father will come to thee soon;
Rest, rest, on mother's breast,
Father will come to thee soon;
Father will come to his babe in the nest,
Silver sails all out of the west,
    Under the silver moon:
Sleep, my little one, sleep, my pretty one, sleep.

(Tennyson: 'Sweet and Low')

Exercises

1. Write a poem describing a journey – by train, by horse, by spaceship, or whatever – using the rhythm of the words to create an appropriate feeling of motion.

2. Write a poem with extra lines just for rhythm, like "fol dee riddle dee dum" and so on.

3. Write a lullaby of your own, or, by contrast, a loud piece to chant like fans on the football terraces – or both.

4. Experiment further with haikus.

5. Read the following first two verses of a poem by A.A. Milne, then write two more verses of your own, following the rhythmic pattern exactly. (The poem is called 'Bad Sir Brian Botany', if you want to look it up later and see how it actually ends.)

> Sir Brian had a battleaxe with great big knobs on;
> He went among the villagers and blipped them on the head.
> On Wednesday and Saturday, but mostly on the latter day,
> He called at all the cottages, and this is what he said:
> > 'I am Sir Brian!' (ting-ling)
> > 'I am Sir Brian!' (rat-tat)
> > 'I am Sir Brian, as bold as a lion –
> > Take that! – and that! – and that!'
>
> Sir Brian had a pair of boots with great big spurs on,
> A fighting pair of which he was particularly fond.
> On Tuesday and on Friday, just to make the street look tidy,
> He'd collect the passing villagers and kick them in the pond.
> > 'I am Sir Brian!' (sper-lash!)
> > 'I am Sir Brian!' (sper-losh!)
> > 'I am Sir Brian, as bold as a lion –
> > Is anyone else for a wash?'

7. Think of any tune or piece of music and write words to fit its rhythm, then sing what you've written.

6
RHYME

Rhyme is so common in poetry, especially traditional poetry, that it is easy to assume that all poetry has to rhyme. Ask most people to write a poem, and they will almost instinctively try to write verses which rhyme.

We are so familiar with rhyme that we can even use it to unravel the sound of new words. Do you know what kr. is short for? You will when you've read this poem!

> She frowned and called him Mr.
> Because in sport he kr.
> And so in spite
> That very nite
> This Mr. kr. sr.

> *(Anon)*

But the purpose of rhyme is only to help create a musical effect. Sometimes, we use the term "verse" to describe a kind of poetry which usually rhymes, and so is fairly musical, but doesn't necessarily have the same word power or concentrated imagery as other poetry.

From your own days as a small child you can probably remember two important things about rhyme – it makes things easier to remember, and it seems to give words extra strength in charms, spells and so on.

Some of the first poems we ever hear as children are nursery rhymes. Can you remember how these continue?:

> Humpty Dumpty sat on a wall . . .

> Baa baa, black sheep . . .

> Hickory dickory dock . . .

> Jack be nimble . . .

> Twinkle, twinkle, little star . . .

Many of these old nursery rhymes, with familiar tunes, are based on events which have long since been forgotten. For example, this is an apparently simple children's game song:

> Ring a ring o' roses,
> A pocketful o' posies;
> Atishoo! Atishoo!
> We all fall down.

But in fact, the song refers to the time of the Great Plague in the seventeenth century, when the first sign of having caught the disease was a ring of red blisters under the armpit, followed by uncontrollable sneezing – death soon followed.

Similarly, this is a traditional children's favourite:

> Half a pound of tuppenny rice,
> Half a pound of treacle,
> Mix it up and make it nice,
> Pop goes the weasel!
>
> Up and down the City Road,
> In and out the Eagle,
> That's the way the money goes,
> Pop goes the weasel!

In fact, "weasel" was a slang word used by London hat-makers in the nineteenth century to describe their personal belongings, and to "pop" the weasel was to take your belongings to the pawnbroker to get enough money to get drunk with. "Treacle" originally comes from a Greek word, "theriake", meaning "an antidote to the poison of wild beasts", and in this poem it means drugs or alcoholic drink. The Eagle was a popular sign for an inn or tavern. So the children's rhyme is nowhere near as innocent as it seems!

As children, we used rhyme to give extra strength to our chants, spells and insults:

> Sticks and stones
> May break my bones,
> But names will never hurt me . . .
>
> Rain, rain, go away,
> Come again another day . . .
>
> Matthew, Mark, Luke and John,
> Bless the bed that I lie on . . .

41

THE POETRY LIBRARY

And we still use rhymes to help remember information. Do you know how these old sayings continue?:

> Red sky at night,
> Shepherd's delight;
> Red sky . . .

> Thirty days hath September,
> April, June . . .

> Monday's child is fair of face,
> Tuesday's child is full of grace,
> Wednesday's child is full of woe,
> Thursday's child . . .

As with rhythm, there are patterns of rhyme which are found in poetry throughout the ages.

Perhaps the most common form of rhyming poetry has four-line verses or **quatrains** with only the second and fourth lines rhyming, like this:

> Lean out of the window,
>   Goldenhair,
> I heard you singing
>   A merry air.
>
> My book is closed;
>   I read no more,
> Watching the fire dance
>   On the floor.
>
> I have left my book;
>   I have left my room,
> For I heard you singing
>   Through the gloom.

> (James Joyce)

Some poems have every three lines rhyming:

The Eagle

He clasps the crag with crooked hands;
Close to the sun in lonely lands,
Ringed with the azure world, he stands.

The wrinkled sea beneath him crawls;
He watches from his mountain walls,
And like a thunderbolt he falls.

(Tennyson)

We sometimes use a letter code to demonstrate the pattern or **rhyme scheme** of a poem. Starting with "a" for the word at the end of the first line, we look at all the other line endings; if a word at the end of a line rhymes with a previous word, it has the same letter, if not, the next letter in the alphabet. The rhyme scheme of the 'The Eagle', for example, is:

a
a
a

b
b
b

A longer and more complicated poem might have a more complicated rhyme scheme, perhaps something like this:

. . .	hand;	a
. . .	giver,	b
. . .	understand,	a
. . .	river.	b
. . .	free,	c
. . .	blown;	d
. . .	be	c
. . .	grown.	d
. . .	time,	e
. . .	sand;	a
. . .	crime.	e
. . .	sight,	f
. . .	stone;	d
. . .	write.	f

43

Humorous verse often rhymes in pairs of lines, or **couplets**. Here's a typical example by the American humorous poet, Ogden Nash:

Tableau at Twilight

I sit in the dusk. I am all alone.
Enter a child and an ice-cream cone.

A parent is easily beguiled
By sight of this coniferous child.

The friendly embers warmer gleam,
The cone begins to drip ice-cream.

Cones are composed of many a vitamin.
My lap is not the place to pitamin.

Although my raiment is not chinchilla,
I flinch to see it become vanilla.

Coniferous child, when vanilla melts
I'd rather it melted somewhere elts.

Exit child with remains of cone.
I sit in the dusk. I am all alone,

Muttering spells like an angry Druid,
Alone, in the dusk, with the cleaning fluid.

A traditional kind of humorous verse uses place names for the first rhyming words in the couplets, like this:

I went to Noke,
But nobody spoke;
I went to Thame,
It was just the same;
Burford and Brill
Were silent and still;
But I went to Beckley
And they spoke directly . . .

Another very famous traditional use of rhyme is in the special London slang known as cockney rhyming slang. A rhyming phrase is substituted for the word, as in "plates of meat" for "feet", or "boat race" (sometimes "Chevy Chase") for "face". Eventually, the actual rhyming word is left off, which can make life very confusing. You might hear someone talk about emptying his "sky" and taking off his "daisies" before going up the "apples" to bed ("sky" = sky-rocket, pocket; "daisies" = daisy roots, boots; "apples" = apples and pears, stairs).

If the rhyming words in a poem are only one syllable long or *monosyllables*, then the rhyme is called *single* or *masculine*, for example, "board" and "hoard", "bent" and "sent". If the rhyming words have two rhyming syllables at the end, that kind of rhyme is called *double* or *feminine*, for example, "treasure" and "pleasure", "enjoying" and "destroying".

Sometimes two words sound similar enough to make a pleasant or effective sound, even though they don't actually rhyme – "time" and "nine", for example. This is called *assonance*. Here's another example, from Lord Tennyson's poem about the Charge of the Light Brigade:

> Half a league, half a league,
>   Half a league *onward*,
> All in the Valley of Death
>   Rode the six *hundred*.

Finally, there is another kind of rhyme which is less than full rhyme, but more than assonance. Not surprisingly, it's called *half-rhyme*. In the following poem by William Shakespeare, look very closely at all the rhyming words.

> Under the greenwood tree,
> Who loves to lie with me,
> And tune his merry note
> Unto the sweet bird's throat,
> Come hither, come hither, come hither:
>   Here shall he see
>   No enemy
> But winter and rough weather.

You will have noticed that "hither" and "weather" don't rhyme exactly, because the internal vowel sound is different.

Here's another example:

> Leaves
>   Murmuring by myriads in the shimmering trees.
> Lives
>   Waking with wonder in the Pyrenees.
> Birds
>   Cheerily chirping in the early day.
> Bards
>   Singing of summer scything through the hay.
> Bees
>   Shaking the heavy dews from bloom and frond.
> Boys
>   Bursting the surface of the ebony pond.
> Flashes
>   Of swimmers carving thro' the sparkling cold.
> Fleshes
>   Gleaming with wetness to the morning gold.

(Wilfred Owen)

The words at the ends of the lines ("trees", "Pyrenees", etc.) are full rhymes; the single words at the beginnings of the lines ("leaves", "lives", etc.) are half-rhymes.

In writing your own poems, you may discover the one great danger in rhyme: beginners often concentrate so hard on finding rhyming words that they forget all the other things they're trying to do in the poem. It's very easy to choose a word you don't really want just because it's the only rhyme you can think of. This sort of thing:

> I was walking my dog
> When I saw a frog
> Sitting on a log.
> It was in a bog.
> Then we had a snog.

Unless you're deliberately choosing daft rhymes for comic effect, be very careful about using rhyme, because once you start it's very difficult to stop! Don't use rhyme just for its own sake, and don't choose a word for the end of a line just because it happens to rhyme – it might not be exactly the word you want, or it might not even make sense. After all:

> Roses are red,
> Violets are blue,
> Some poems rhyme,
> This one doesn't!

Exercises

1. Write a poem of six lines in which the first three lines all rhyme, and the second three lines all rhyme, in other words with the rhyme scheme:

     a
     a
     a

     b
     b
     b

2. Continue this poem for as long as you can (about 40 lines would be very impressive!) making every line carry on the "street" rhyme, but not using any rhyming word more than *once*:

     I met a man in the street
     whose big hairy feet
     smelled pleasant and sweet
     despite the great heat . . .

3. Write a poem in couplets, using local or national place names to end the first line of each couplet. For example:

     I went to Redruth;
     They told the truth.
     I went to St. Ives
     And married two wives . . .

4. The words in the left-hand column below are all half-rhymes with the words in the right-hand column, but the order is jumbled. First match the rhyming pairs, then use them to end the lines of a ten-line poem:

     green   sheep
     tell   droves
     drives   angry
     hungry   grown
     shape   till

5. Read some more poems by Ogden Nash, then have a go at writing your own humorous poems in rhyming couplets. Or try writing a pantomime scene, again using rhyming couplets, just like in traditional pantomime.

6. Find a poem in a book and describe its rhyme scheme to the rest of the class.

7. Find out more about cockney rhyming slang and tell the class about it.

8. Try to find out more about the origin of nursery rhymes.

7

DESCRIBING POEMS – 1 OBJECTS AND ANIMALS

Many poems are not written to tell a story – they are simply meant to describe something, but in an unusual or exciting way. Here, for example, is a description of the Moon and stars on an autumn night:

> A touch of cold in the Autumn night –
> I walked abroad,
> And saw the ruddy Moon lean over a hedge
> Like a red-faced farmer.
> I did not stop to speak, but nodded,
> And round about were the wistful stars
> With white faces like town children.

> *(T.E. Hulme)*

The Moon is *like* a farmer and the stars are *like* children – the poet is comparing one thing with another. This kind of comparison is called a *simile*. Other examples are: "as white as snow", "like the red balloon", "as old as the hills", "like the sea", and so on.

Sometimes the poet goes even further and talks as if the thing he is describing actually *is* something else, even though we all know it isn't. He might say "the sea dances" or "the Moon sails across the sea of night", as if the sea actually were a dancer and the Moon actually were a ship. This kind of comparison is called a *metaphor*. It is one of the most common and most powerful devices in poetry. If you want to be a good poet, effective use of metaphor is the most important skill you need to acquire.

Often the poet describes what he has seen, but also tells us some of his thoughts about it:

> I wander'd lonely as a cloud
> That floats on high o'er vales and hills,
> When all at once I saw a crowd,
> A host, of golden daffodils;
> Beside the lake, beneath the trees,
> Fluttering and dancing in the breeze.

Continuous as the stars that shine
And twinkle on the Milky Way,
They stretch'd in never-ending line
Along the margin of a bay:
Ten thousand saw I at a glance
Tossing their heads in sprightly dance.

The waves beside them danced, but they
Out-did the sparkling waves in glee:
A poet could not but be gay
In such a jocund company:
I gazed – and gazed – but little thought
What wealth to me the show had brought:

For oft, when on my couch I lie
In vacant or in pensive mood,
They flash upon that inward eye
Which is the bliss of solitude;
And then my heart with pleasure fills,
And dances with the daffodils.

(William Wordsworth)

The most successful describing poems are ones which bring out details so clearly that you can almost see, or hear, or feel, or smell what is being described. Here the Scottish poet Hugh MacDiarmid describes a pigeon's skull which he has found on the "machair" or moor:

I found a pigeon's skull on the machair,
All the bones pure white and dry, and chalky,
But perfect,
Without a crack or a flaw anywhere.

At the back, rising out of the beak,
Were domes like bubbles of thin bone,
Almost transparent, where the brain had been
That fixed the tilt of the wings.

Here is a rather more joyful poem about an Irish terrier called Tim:

It's wonderful dogs they're breeding now:
Small as a flea or large as a cow;
But my old lad Tim he'll never be bet
By any dog that ever he met.
"Come on," says he, "for I'm not kilt yet!"

No matter the size of the dog he'll meet,
Tim trails his coat the length o' the street.
D'ye mind his scars an' his ragged ear,
The like of a Dublin Fusilier?
He's a massacree dog that knows no fear.

But he'd stick to me till his latest breath;
An' he'd go with me to the gates of death.
He'd wait for a thousand years, maybe,
Scratching the door and whining for me
If myself were inside in Purgatory.

So I laugh when I hear thim make it plain
That dogs and men never meet again.
For all their talk, who'd listen to thim,
With the soul in the shining eyes of him?
Would God be wasting a dog like Tim?

(Winifred M. Letts)

The two main elements in good descriptive poetry are, firstly, close and very accurate observation of what is being described, and, secondly, vivid and colourful recreation of the experience. In the following poem, look very closely at the descriptive metaphors.

Little flocks of peaceful clouds,
    Lying in your fields so blue,
While my eyes look up they see
    A black Ram coming close to you.

He will scatter you poor flocks,
    He will tear up north and south;
Lightning will come from his eye,
    And fierce thunder from his mouth.

Little flocks of peaceful clouds,
    Soon there'll be a dreadful rout;
That Ram's horns can toss big ships,
    Tear an oak tree's bowels out.

(W.H. Davies)

What actually is the black ram? What are the clouds compared to? Precisely which words create the metaphors and images in the poem?

Finally, here is a slightly longer poem packed with brilliant descriptive detail:

The Fish

I caught a tremendous fish
and held him beside the boat
half out of water, with my hook
fast in a corner of his mouth.
He didn't fight.
He hadn't fought at all.
He hung a grunting weight,
battered and venerable
and homely. Here and there
his brown skin hung in strips
like ancient wallpaper,
and its pattern of darker brown
was like wallpaper:
shapes like full-blown roses
stained and lost through age.
He was speckled with barnacles,
fine rosettes of lime,
and infested
with tiny white sea-lice,
and underneath two or three
rags of green weed hung down.
While his gills were breathing in
the terrible oxygen
– the frightening gills,
fresh and crisp with blood,
that can cut so badly –
I thought of the coarse white flesh
packed in like feathers,
the big bones and the little bones,
the dramatic reds and blacks
and the pink swim-bladder
like a big peony.
I looked into his eyes
which were far larger than mine
but shallower, and yellowed,
the irises backed and packed
with tarnished tinfoil
seen through the lenses
of old scratched isinglass.

They shifted a little, but not
to return my stare.
– It was more like the tipping
of an object toward the light.
I admired his sullen face,
the mechanism of his jaw,
and then I saw
that from his lower lip
– if you could call it a lip –
grim, wet, and weaponlike,
hung five old pieces of fish-line,
or four and a wire leader
with the swivel still attached,
with all their five big hooks
grown firmly in his mouth.
A green line, frayed at the end
where he broke it, two heavier lines,
and a fine black thread
still crimped from the strain and snap
when it broke and he got away.

Like medals with their ribbons
frayed and wavering,
a five-haired beard of wisdom
trailing from his aching jaw.
I stared and stared
and victory filled up
the little rented boat,
from the pool of bilge
where oil had spread a rainbow
around the rusted engine
to the bailer rusted orange,
the sun-cracked thwarts,
the oarlocks on their strings,
the gunnels – until everything
was rainbow, rainbow, rainbow!
And I let the fish go.

(Elizabeth Bishop)

Exercises

1. Find an interesting object (or photograph) to describe. First list all the details in note form. Next add any *similes* which occur to you (for example, "the skin is wrinkled . . . like the bark of an old tree"). Finally, change some of your similes to *metaphors* or write new metaphors. Now shape eveything you've written into a descriptive poem.

2. Make a long list of similes or metaphors comparing the Moon with other objects ("like a silver coin" . . . "a great round cheese" etc.) then arrange your best phrases to make a poem. Try to find comparisons you don't think other people will have made before.

3. Do the same for the Sun.

4. Write a poem of about ten or twelve lines describing any of the following. Try to see, hear, smell, taste and feel the thing in your mind. Don't worry about rhyme, just concentrate on noticing and describing. Start a new line for each new detail, or when the rhythm feels right.

   a farmyard   an old rowing boat   a tree   a messy kitchen   an old brick wall   an ashtray   a fast car   a deserted house

5. Write a poem describing any of the following animals. Try to get across an idea of the animal's character and life as well as what it looks like. Choose words for the animal's movements and noises especially carefully:

a cockerel a Jersey cow a piglet an old carthorse a kitten a guide-dog an elephant a snake a wolf-cub an ant

6. Write a poem about one of your pets.

7. Find a painting or photograph which really appeals to you. Try to reproduce what you see and what you feel in a poem.

8
DESCRIBING POEMS 2 – PEOPLE

When a poet describes people, he has to include their feelings and attitudes, as well as what they look and sound like. Part of the following poem about a schoolboy is physical description, but mostly the poem is telling us what Timothy Winters is like as a person:

Timothy Winters comes to school
With eyes as wide as a football-pool,
Ears like bombs and teeth like splinters:
A blitz of a boy is Timothy Winters.

His belly is white, his neck is dark,
And is hair is an exclamation-mark.
His clothes are enough to scare a crow
And through his britches the blue winds blow.

When teacher talks he won't hear a word
And he shoots down dead the arithmetic bird,
He licks the patterns off his plate,
And he's not even heard of the Welfare State.

Timothy Winters has bloody feet
And he lives in a house on Suez Street,
He sleeps in a sack on the kitchen floor
And they say there aren't boys like him any more.

Old Man Winters likes his beer
And his missus ran off with a bombadier,
Grandma sits in the grate with a gin
And Timothy's dosed with an aspirin.

The Welfare Worker lies awake
But the law's as tricky as a ten-foot snake,
So Timothy Winters drinks his cup
And slowly goes on growing up.

At morning prayers the Master helves
For children less fortunate than ourselves,
And the loudest response in the room is when
Timothy Winters roars "Amen!"

So come one angel, come on ten:
Timothy Winters says "Amen
Amen amen amen amen."
Timothy Winters, Lord.
        Amen.

(Charles Causley)

A good poem about a person does the same as a good painting or photographic portrait – it gives us lots of interesting and convincing detail, but more importantly it thrusts the person's unique character strongly and clearly into our minds. Noticing small details is important (like Timothy Winters sleeping in a sack) because it helps bring characters to life; such details can often be very revealing.

Here are some very short descriptive extracts from a number of different poems describing people. Notice how they capture the mood or attitude of the people they are describing:

> . . . my father's pages rustle, he makes himself a nest of newspaper . . .

> . . . old men with closed faces . . .

> . . . starless and old and blind, a sight for pity, with feeble steps and fingers on the wall gropes with his staff . . .

> . . . a heap of verminous rags and matted hair . . .

> . . . his beard as any sow or fox was red, and thereto broad, as though it were a spade . . . his mouth as great was as a great furnace . . .

> . . . whimpering like a stricken animal . . .

> . . . by God, the old man could handle a spade . . .

> . . . I'm a right old criminal, dead smart, one of the boys . . .

. . . the whining school-boy, with his satchel and
shining morning face, creeping like snail unwillingly
to school . . .

The following two poems are both about somebody who is now dead. ('In Memoriam' means "in memory of".) This kind of poem is called an *elegy*. Elegies used to be written only for the great and famous, praising their magnificent achievements, but V.C. Horwell's poem is about a very ordinary man:

In Memoriam: Alf Butterworth

A helpful boy,
Carrying coal from the shed, salt to the larder,
Bread from the shop.

In steady work,
Making keys for doorlocks, labels for jamjars,
Wheels for field-guns.

Her thrifty man,
Saving coupons for plates, crates for kindling,
Sops for his hens.

Our kindly dad,
Giving annuals at Christmas, bikes to the big boy,
Rene at the church.

Through peaceful age,
Writing minutes for the club, letters to the council,
Cards to grandsons.

Died on Saturday, while standing at the bus-stop,
Next to Rene's boy Terry, who was bringing home the bread.

Tony Connor's elegy is for an old plumber called Alfred Hubbard. It tells us the bad things about him as well as the good:

Hubbard is dead, the old plumber;
who will mend our burst pipes now,
the tap that has dripped all the summer,
testing the sink's overflow?

No other like him. Young men with knowledge
of new techniques, theories from books,
may better his work straight from college,
but who will challenge his squint-eyed looks

in kitchen, bathroom, under-floorboards,
rules of thumb which were often wrong;
seek as erringly stopcocks in cupboards,
or make a job last half as long?

He was a man who knew the ginnels,
alleyways, streets – the whole district,
family secrets, minor annals,
time-honoured fictions fused to fact.

Seventy years of gossip muttered
under his cap, his tufty thatch,
so that his talk was slow and clotted,
hard to follow, and too much.

As though nothing fell, none vanished,
and time were the maze of Cheetham Hill,
in which the dead – with jobs unfinished –
waited to hear him ring the bell.

For much he never got round to doing,
but meant to, when weather bucked up,
or worsened, or when his pipe was drawing,
or when he'd finished this cup.

I thought time, he forgot so often,
had forgotten him, but here's Death's pomp
over his house, and by the coffin
the son who will inherit his blowlamp,

tools, workshop, cart, and cornet
(pride of Cheetham Prize Brass Band),
and there's his mourning widow, Janet,
stood at the gate he'd promised to mend.

Soon he will make his final journey;
shaved and silent, strangely trim,
with never a pause to talk to any-
body: how arrow-like, for him!

In St. Mark's Church, whose dismal tower
he pointed and painted when a lad,
they will sing his praises amidst flowers
while somewhere, a cellar starts to flood,

and the housewife banging his front-door knocker
is not surprised to find him gone,
and runs for Thwaite, who's a better worker,
and sticks at a job until it's done.

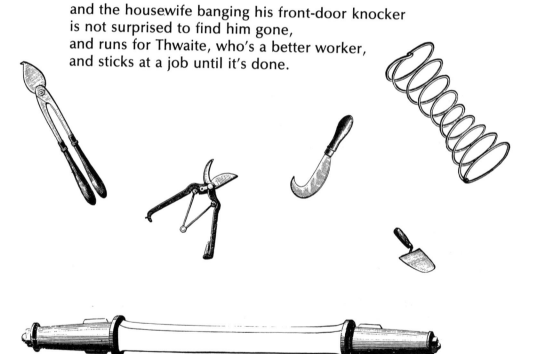

Exercises

1. Imagine you are a local newspaper reporter. Write a newspaper account (obituary) of the death of Alf Butterworth, using the information given and implied in V.C. Horwell's poem.

2. Read 'Elegy for Alfred Hubbard' again carefully. Write a list in two columns, with all Alfred's good points on one side and all his bad points on the other.

3. Write a short story with either Timothy Winters, Alf Butterworth or Alfred Hubbard as the main character.

4. Write an elegy for somebody who is now dead – either somebody you knew personally, or somebody famous.

5. Write a poem describing someone you know in school. If it's not very flattering, make sure it's not about someone who might recognise your description and punch you on the nose!

6. Write a poem describing one of your neighbours or relatives. Remember to describe the person's feelings and attitudes as well as what he or she looks like and does.

7. Choose any of the following and write a poem about them:

a tramp	a young businessman
a refugee	a handicapped child
a policeman	an old fisherman
an athlete	a factory girl
a hunter	a dentist
a punk rocker	a wizard
a knight	a pop star
a bully	a foreigner
a mad scientist	an old lady

9
POEMS FOR MORE THAN ONE VOICE

Many poems contain words spoken by more than one voice.

With a partner, practise speaking aloud this poem by Christina Rossetti, with one of you as the ferryman and the other as the passenger:

> 'Ferry me across the water,
>   Do, boatman, do.'
> 'If you've a penny in your purse,
>   I'll ferry you.'
>
> 'I have a penny in my purse,
>   And my eyes are blue;
> So ferry me across the water,
>   Do, boatman, do.'

'Step into my ferry-boat,
    Be they black or blue,
And for the penny in your purse
    I'll ferry you.'

The traditional poem 'The Keeper' is also well known as a folk song. Practise saying or singing the words in a group, sharing out who says what in the way you think best:

Verse: The keeper did a-shooting go,
         And under his cloak he carried a bow
         All for to shoot at a merry little doe,
             Among the leaves so green, O!

Chorus: Jackie boy!
                              Master!
         Sing ye well?
                              Very well.
         Hey down!
                              Ho down!
             Derry derry down,
             Among the leaves so green, O!
         To my hey down down!
                              To my ho down down!
         Hey down!
                              Ho down!
             Derry derry down,
             Among the leaves so green, O!

Verse: The first doe he shot at he missed,
         The second doe he trimmed, he kissed,
         The third doe went where nobody wist
             Among the leaves so green, O!

         (Chorus)

         The fourth doe she did cross the plain;
         The keeper fetched her back again;
         Where she is now she may remain,
             Among the leaves so green, O!

         (Chorus)

The fifth doe she did cross the brook;
The keeper fetched her back with his crook;
Where she is now you must go and look,
　　Among the leaves so green, O!

(Chorus)

The sixth doe she ran over the plain;
But he with his hounds did turn her again,
And it's there he did hunt in a merry, merry vein,
　　Among the leaves so green, O!

(Chorus)

Jonathan Swift, in his poem 'A Gentle Echo on Woman', uses the voice of an echo to make some jokes about how men should treat women:

Shepherd:　Echo, I ween, will in the word reply,
　　　　　　And quaintly answer questions; shall I try?

Echo:　　　　　　　　　　　　　　　　　　Try.

Shepherd:　What must we do our passion to express?

Echo:　　　　　　　　　　　　　　　　　　Press.

Shepherd:　What most moves women when we them address?

Echo:　　　　　　　　　　　　　　　　　　A dress.

Shepherd:　If music softens rocks, love tunes my lyre.

Echo:　　　　　　　　　　　　　　　　　　Liar.

Shepherd:　Then teach me, Echo, how shall I come by her?

Echo:　　　　　　　　　　　　　　　　　　Buy her.

Shepherd:　When bought, no question I shall be her dear?

Echo:　　　　　　　　　　　　　　　　　　Her deer.

Shepherd:　But what can glad me when she's laid on bier?

Echo:　　　　　　　　　　　　　　　　　　Beer.

Shepherd:　What must I do when women will be kind?

Echo:　　　　　　　　　　　　　　　　　　Be kind.

Shepherd:　What must I do when women will be cross?

Echo:　　　　　　　　　　　　　　　　　　Be cross.

Shepherd: Lord, what is she that can so turn and wind?

Echo: Wind.

Shepherd: If she be wind, what stills her when she blows?

Echo: Blows.

Shepherd: But if she bang again, still should I bang her?

Echo: Bang her.

Shepherd: Is there no way to moderate her anger?

Echo: Hang her.

Shepherd: Thanks, gentle Echo! right thy answers tell
What woman is and how to guard her well.

Echo: Guard her well.

There have, of course, been many plays written in poetry and verse, from the ancient Greek tragedies right through to modern plays and pantomimes. (Shakespeare, incidentally, occasionally wrote rhyming lines as well as blank verse, particularly in the early plays and comedies.) Most modern pantomimes still keep the tradition of the fairy and other magical creatures like wizards speaking in rhyming verse.

Perhaps the most famous modern play written in poetry is T.S. Eliot's *'Murder in the Cathedral'*, which is about the true story of the murder of Thomas Becket, Archbishop of Canterbury. In this short extract, Thomas meets for the first time the knights who have come on the King's orders to murder him:

Thomas: You say, from the King?

First Knight: Most surely, from the King.
We must speak with you alone.

Thomas (to Priests):   Leave us then alone.
Now what is the matter?

First Knight: This is the matter.

The Three Knights: You are the Archbishop in revolt against the
King; in rebellion to the King and the law of the
land;
You are the Archbishop who was made by the
King; whom he set in your place to carry out
his command.
You are his servant, his tool, and his jack,
You wore his favours on your back,
You had your honours all from his hand; from
him you had the power, the seal and the ring.
This is the man who was the tradesman's son:
the backstairs brat who was born in Cheapside;
This is the creature that crawled upon the King;
   swollen with blood and swollen with pride.
Creeping out of the London dirt,
Crawling up like a louse on your shirt,
The man who cheated, swindled, lied; broke
his oath and betrayed his King.

Exercises

1. Write a poem for two voices, concentrating on rhythm and balance between the voices. Practise it with a partner, then speak it for the rest of the class.

2. Write a poem to be spoken by three or more people, clearly labelling which lines are to be spoken by whom.

3. Write an echo poem.

4. Write a short play, or a scene from a play, in verse.

10
CHARMS AND SPELLS

Because poetry uses powerful words in a concentrated way, it is often used in magic ceremonies, rituals, spells, charms and curses.

Here are two ancient charms. The first is for wealth – you are supposed to throw the nine named objects down a well whilst saying:

> Three white stones,
> And three black pins,
> Three yellow daisies
> Off the green,
>
> Into the well,
> With a one, two, three,
> And a fortune, a fortune,
> Come to me.

The second charm is to remove warts from the hands – you are supposed to wash your hands in the Moon's rays shining in a dry metal basin and say:

> I wash my hands in this thy dish,
> Oh, Man in the Moon, do grant my wish,
> And come and take away this.

Here is an unpleasant charm; it is a spell to destroy life which was used traditionally by the Cherokee Indians of North America:

Listen!

Now I have come to step over your soul
(I know your clan)
(I know your name)
(I have stolen your spit and buried it under earth)
I bury your soul under earth
I cover you over with black rock
I cover you over with black cloth
I cover you over with black slabs
You disappear for ever
Your path leads to the
Black Coffin
in the hills of the darkening land

So let it be for you

The clay of the hills covers you
the black clay of the Darkening Land

Your soul fades away

It becomes blue
When darkness comes your spirit shrivels
and dwindles to disappear for ever

Listen!

But not all charms are unpleasant. This charm, from Shakespeare's play 'A Midsummer Night's Dream', is spoken to protect the Queen of the Fairies as she lies sleeping. It was probably sung as a song when it was performed in Shakespeare's time:

> You spotted snakes, with double tongue,
> Thorny hedgehogs, be not seen;
> Newts and blind-worms, do no wrong;
> Come not near our fairy queen;
> Philomel, with melody
> Sing in our sweet lullaby;
> Lulla, lulla, lullaby; lulla, lulla, lullaby;
> Never harm, nor spell nor charm
> Come our lovely lady nigh;
> So, goodnight, with lullaby.
>
> Weaving spiders, come not here;
> Hence, you long-legged spinners, hence;
> Beetles, black, approach not near;
> Worm, nor snail, do no offence.
> Philomel, with melody
> Sing in our sweet lullaby;
> Lulla, lulla, lullaby; lulla, lulla, lullaby;
> Never harm, nor spell nor charm
> Come our lovely lady nigh;
> So, goodnight, with lullaby.

Compare that peaceful charm with this witches' spell from another of Shakespeare's plays, 'Macbeth':

> First Witch: Round about the cauldron go;
> In the poison'd entrails throw.
> Toad, that under cold stone
> Days and nights hast thirty-one
> Swelter'd venom sleeping got,
> Boil thou first i' the charmed pot.
>
> All: Double, double toil and trouble;
> Fire, burn; and, cauldron, bubble.

Second Witch: Fillet of a fenny snake,
              In the cauldron boil and bake;
              Eye of newt, and toe of frog,
              Wool of bat, and tongue of dog,
              Adder's fork, and blind-worm's sting,
              Lizard's leg, and howlet's wing,
              For a charm of powerful trouble;
              Like a hell-broth boil and bubble.

       All: Double, double toil and trouble;
             Fire, burn; and, cauldron, bubble.

Third Witch: Scale of dragon, tooth of wolf,
              Witches' mummy, maw and gulf
              Of the ravin'd salt-sea shark,
              Root of hemlock digg'd i' the dark,
              Liver of blaspheming Jew,
              Gall of goat, and slips of yew
              Sliver'd in the moon's eclipse,
              Nose of Turk, and Tartar's lips,
              Finger of birth-strangled babe
              Ditch-deliver'd by a drab,
              Make the gruel thick and slab:
              Add thereto a tiger's chaudron,
              For the ingredients of our cauldron.

       All: Double, double toil and trouble;
             Fire, burn; and, cauldron, bubble.

Second Witch: Cool it with a baboon's blood,
               Then the charm is firm and good.

Exercises

1. Write a spell to make it rain, the kind that might be chanted by a witch-doctor or a medicine man.

2. Write a charm or spell to cure someone of an illness.

3. Imagine you are a modern witch around a modern (microwave!) cauldron. Make a poem listing all the horrible things you would throw in it.

4. The following lines begin a traditional Irish blessing. Add six more lines of your own, each line beginning with "May . . ."

> May the blessing of light be with you –
>   light outside and light within.
> May sunlight shine upon you and warm your heart
>   till it glows like a great peat fire
> so that the stranger may come and warm himself at it.
> May a blessed light shine out of your two eyes
>   like a candle set in two windows of a house,
>   bidding the wanderer to come out of the storm.

5. Find out more about traditional charm and spell poems, then tell the class what you have discovered.

11
EXPERIMENTS 1 – PUNCTUATION AND NEW WORDS

You will already have noticed that poetry is usually written in short lines, with the traditional convention being that a capital letter is used at the beginning of each line, like this:

> You will already have noticed
> That poetry is usually written
> In short lines,
> With the traditional convention being
> That a capital letter is used
> At the beginning of each line,
> Like this!

Many modern poets still write in short lines, but either write with normal standard punctuation, even at the beginning of the line, or abandon normal punctuation altogether, perhaps something like this:

> you say
> you have no home
> to go to
> well
> that's what
> you say
>
> I say
> here's your home
> wherever
> I am

Sometimes poets work so hard at describing things in a new, concentrated way that they stretch language itself into new shapes, inventing or *coining* new words and finding new ways of using punctuation.

Here is a poem deliberately written without punctuation; the words drift together in small clusters just like debris in the broken-down spacecraft which the poem describes:

Spacepoem 3 : Off Course

the golden flood   the weightless seat
the cabin song   the pitch black
the growing beard   the floating crumb
the shining rendezvous   the orbit wisecrack
the hot spacesuit   the smuggled mouth-organ
the imaginary somersault   the visionary sunrise
the turning continents   the space debris
the golden lifeline   the space walk
the crawling deltas   the camera moon
the pitch velvet   the rough sleep
the crackling headphone   the space silence
the turning earth   the lifeline continents
the cabin sunrise   the hot flood
the shining spacesuit   the growing moon
   the crackling somersault   the smuggled orbit
   the rough moon   the visionary rendezvous
   the weightless headphone   the cabin debris
   the floating lifeline   the pitch sleep
   the crawling camera   the turning silence
   the space crumb   the crackling beard
   the orbit mouth-organ   the floating song

(*Edwin Morgan*)

Here's a poem by e.e. cummings (who always wrote his name without capital letters) which has punctuation, but in most unusual places. How would you read this poem aloud?

Four III

here's a little mouse) and
what does he think about, i
wonder as over this
floor (quietly with

bright eyes) drifts (nobody
can tell because
Nobody knows, or why
jerks Here &, here,
gr(oo)ving the room's Silence) this like
a littlest

poem a
(with wee ears and see?
tail frisks)

        (gonE)
'mouse',
       We are not the same you and

i, since here's a little he
or is
it It
? (or was something we saw in the mirror)?

therefore we'll kiss; for maybe
what was Disappeared
into ourselves
who (look). , startled

Poems with invented words can be great fun. Here's Lewis Carroll's 'Jabberwocky':

'Twas brillig, and the slithy toves
  Did gyre and gimble in the wabe:
All mimsy were the borogroves,
  And the mome raths outgrabe.

'Beware the Jabberwock, my son!
  The jaws that bite, the claws that catch!
Beware the Jubjub bird, and shun
  The frumious Bandersnatch!'

He took his vorpal sword in hand:
  Long time the manxome foe he sought –
So rested he by the Tumtum tree,
  And stood awhile in thought.

And, as in uffish thought he stood,
  The Jabberwock, with eyes of flame,
Came whiffling through the tulgey wood,
  And burbled as it came!

One, two! One, two! And through and through
  The vorpal blade went snicker-snack!
He left it dead, and with its head
  He went galumphing back.

'And hast thou slain the Jabberwock?
  Come to my arms, my beamish boy!
O frabjous day! Callooh! Callay!'
  He chortled in his joy.

'Twas brillig, and the slightly toves
  Did gyre and gimble in the wabe:
All mimsy were the borogroves,
  And the momeraths outgrabe.

Spike Milligan is similarly inventive in this poem:

Ye Tortures

From a document found in the Archives of Bude Monastery during a squirting excavation. It shows a complete list of tortures, approved by the Mistry of Works in the year 1438, for failure to pay leg tithe, or sockage.

The prisoner will be:

Bluned on ye Grunions
   and krelled on his Grotts
Ye legges will be twergled
   and pulled thru' ye motts!

His Nukes will be Fongled
   split thrice on yon Thrulls
Then laid on ye Quottle
   and hung by ye Bhuls!

Twice thocked on the Phneffic,
   Yea broggled thrice twee.
Ye moggs will be grendled
   and stretched six foot three!

By now, if ye victim
   show not ye sorrow,
Send him home. Tell him,
   'Come back tomorrow.'

The English language is so robust, it can stand almost any amount of vigorous handling, including the coining of new words. It's very easy to put parts of words together differently to create new words, like this:

wayfalling . . . downgrope . . . grimtalk . . . fanciwished . . . squidgelet . . . shotgrip . . . crocobite . . . sicktwitch . . . distrail . . . underbind . . . wetlap

What the new words *mean* is a different matter, of course!

Exercises

1. Write a poem in which commas, full stops, question marks, brackets, and so on, are used in an unusual way.

2. Use the following words, all coined by a poet called Gerard Manley Hopkins, in a poem of your own. The approximate meaning is in brackets after each word.

   couple-colour   (dappled, mottled)
   moonmarks   (crescent-shaped marks, like a thin New Moon)
   barrowy   (shaped like a round hill or barrow)
   rutpeel   (hard crusts of dried mud at the edge of a puddle)
   chevy   (to race or scamper)
   burling   (bubbling, pouring out, overflowing)

3. Write a poem in which you use some new words you have invented.

12

EXPERIMENTS 2 – VERSE PATTERNS

As well as experimenting with new words and new ways of using punctuation, many poets experiment with patterns.

A very easy poetry writing game is to write a name or word down the left-hand side of the page and use each letter as the first letter of a line, like this:

> Revving and roaring
> Over the dusty hills on my
> Bike, I bite the dust but
> Every circuit I get faster.
> Racing's what I love to do, and
> Trophies are what I'm after.

Use your own name, or somebody else's, and try to say as much as you can about the person in a few lines. You could try the same thing with the name of a city or a country, like this:

> Plying the river go great wide ships,
> Loaded with cargo, or sailors, or troops,
> Yet gliding with ease through the river's
> Mouth to the wide, calm sea.
> Over the broad water stretch two arms,
> Urging their traffic along; the tall
> Towers of Brunel's bridge for trains, the
> High wires where the motor-car reigns.

You'll sometimes see poems which have two short sets of lines written or printed next to each other, so that you read them from left to right separately and together, like this:

Siege

he peeps   i duck
i shoot   he ducks
i wave   he waves back
i peep   he shoots
he waves   i shoot
and duck   i peep

i peep again

he's dead

           draped across his turret
he smiles   my arrow tickles
the inside of his head

(Johnny Byrne)

Or the poet may spread his text even more widely, as Roger McGough has done in this poem called 'Watchwords':

watch the words
watch words the
watchword is
watch words are
sly as boots
ifyoutakeyoureyesoffthemforaminute

         up

and   they're   and

  away

        allover

     the

        place

Another fun experiment is to write a poem in the shape of the thing you're describing, like these two examples:

when it's raining
when it's hot
whether it's sunny
or weather it's not
I've got
an umbrella's a thing I'm glad

My wretched selfish
sister has eaten
my apple
which
I
gave
her to look
after. I think
she's rotten to the core.

Another interesting way of writing a poem is to tear out a page from an old newspaper or magazine and see if you can "find" a poem hidden in it – you highlight or draw a circle round words or phrases in the order you find them to make a poem:

It has been suggested that there is a zone of comets at the Solar System's edge and **beyond the orbit of Pluto**, from which comets are brought to perihelion from time to **time** by planetary perturbations. This, however, is a question which **has not yet been settled**. The behaviour of comets is interesting. As a rule, comets become observable only when they are less than twice the Earth's distance from the Sun. Whether they will be seen from the Earth depends, of course, on their position in the sky; the most brilliant comets usually appear in the **part of the night** sky above where the Sun is situated. Often, the orientation of a comet's orbit will mean that it is unfavourably placed when at its closest, and it **is easy to miss** the return of a faint periodic comet in this way. On other occasions, it may happen that the combined movements of the Earth and a comet will make the latter appear to stand still against the star background; alternatively, it may appear to be heading directly towards the Earth, or **simply drifting away at an angle**. As the above remarks no doubt make clear, it is possible to observe comets only when they are in the part of their orbit nearest the Sun. There are two reasons for this: they do not become bright enough to be seen until they have come within a certain distance of the Sun, and their orbits may take them **right into the twilight zone** of the Earth's atmosphere, where, of course, they are too faint to be seen.

With the punctuation tidied up, and written out in lines, that "found" text new looks like this:

> Beyond the orbit of Pluto
> time has not yet been settled;
> part of the night is easy to miss,
> simply drifting away at an angle,
> right into the twilight zone.

That example may not be great poetry, but it gives you the idea of how to go about finding poems in old scrap text.

Lastly, you might like to try a poetry writing game called Word Drop. You cut about forty or fifty words out of newspaper headlines then literally throw them up in the air. When they land on the table or floor, you try to arrange them into a poem, using as many as you can.

Exercises

1. Write a few poems using names of people and places to give you the starting letter for each line.

2. Write a poem about and in the shape of any of the following:

   bananas   a spiral staircase
   a rocket   waves
   a waterfall   a spider's web
   a mountain   a racing car

3. Write a poem in any other shape which occurs to you.

4. Write a poem in double columns, with each column making some sort of sense in itself, but also with a meaning going across the lines.

5. Experiment with "found" poems and Word Drop poems.

13
GENERAL WORKSHOP

Here are some general ideas for extending your poetry writing practice:

1. In pairs or in small groups, choose a subject you want to write a poem about. Agree on a title, if you wish. Write your first draft on your own. When you have finished, give your poem to your partner, or to someone else in the group, to read. Read the poem your partner gives you, marking the words or phrases which you think are most effective. Tell your partner which bits you liked, which bits you disliked or couldn't understand, and give reasons if you can. Swap poems again, and re-write your own poem, trying to improve it. Either repeat the process until everybody in the group is happy with his or her poem, or work as a group to combine all the good words and phrases into one group poem.

2. Find a photograph of someone in an old newspaper or magazine and cut it out. Write a poem speaking to the reader in that person's voice. Pin the picture to your poem and display them together. Ask other people what they think the person might be saying.

3. With a partner, or in a group, have a brainstorming session on a particular topic, simply trying to gather as many words and phrases as you can. List your words under useful headings, as in the example given below on "Fireworks". Use the material you have collected in a poem, either as a group or individually.

FIREWORKS **Description**: shooting sparks; spiralling threads of crimson, columns of jades and yellows; coil of lights; flash of brightness; irridescent haze; like a string of multi-coloured beads; trickles of smoke; dazzling rays; stream of sparks; haze of whirling lights; spark shower; glittering; glowing; sparkling; golden.

Sounds: fizzing; hiss; zip; drum-roll; crackling twigs; gush; whoosh; rattle; clack; splutter; twang; muffle; snap; clap; thump; boom; toot; smack; whoop; clamour; bellow; sigh; howl; shriek; whinny; yap; gurgle; wail; hum; snarl.

Movement: twirl; twist; spiralling; whirl; encircling; revolve; gyrate; float; swivel; swirl; coil; spinning; winding; leaping; dancing.

Comparisons: like a burning wand; like a torch; a burning pencil; like a coiled snake; small golden sparks like stars; whirling marigolds; like sudden fiery flowers; a string of irridescent pearls; a rose of fire.

4. Find a story or essay either written by yourself, by someone else in the class, or in an anthology. Write a poem based on the story or inspired by any character or incident in it.

5. Write a poem based on, or inspired by, any book you have read, either in school or at home.

6. Write a poem telling the story of an incident in your early childhood.

7. Using the Library or school books, find three or four poems on the same topic and read them carefully. Discuss them with a partner or your teacher. Then write a poem of your own on the same topic, perhaps with a partner or in a group. Display the original poems and your finished work together.

8. Find a book of paintings or photographs. Write a poem based on any of the pictures.

9. Write a poem based on, or inspired by, any piece of music. Play the music to the class and read your poem to them.

10. Write a poem, either for one voice or several voices, to be tape-recorded with music and/or sound effects.

11. Use still transparencies or your own video recording to illustrate a poem, perhaps with someone reading the poem as a voice-over. Project or play your work to the class.

12. Collect your best work and other good work in the class and edit it into a magazine, either just for your class, or for the whole school.

13. Find out whether there is a Poetry Society or magazine in your area.

14. Find out what your Regional Arts Association is doing about poetry, particularly whether they organise readings by professional poets, or training courses for children and schools, or whether they publish poems in a regional magazine.

15. Find out more about trying to get your poems published by reading the Markets for Verse section in the *Writers' and Artists' Year Book*, published by A. & C. Black Ltd.

GLOSSARY

accent	(see stress)
alliteration	the use of the same letter or group of letters, usually at the beginnings of words, e.g. "*broken bones*"
anonymous	written by an unknown author or poet
assonance	the use of similar vowel and consonant sounds in words, e.g. "onward, hundred"
blank verse	poetry which does not rhyme but which has a clear rhythmical pattern, usually of lines ten syllables long
coining	inventing new words
couplet	poetry verse with two lines, usually rhyming
double rhyme	(see feminine rhyme)
elegy	a poem about someone who is dead
feminine rhyme	rhyme of two syllables, e.g. "treasure . . . pleasure"
haiku	a short Japanese poem with seventeen syllables
half rhyme	pairing of words with the same letters at the beginning and end, but different internal vowel sounds, e.g. "lives . . . loaves"
iambic	a common rhythmical pattern in English poetry of two syllables, the first unstressed, the second stressed, (˘ /): da-DAH, da-DAH, and so on
iambic pentameter	rhythmical pattern found commonly in blank verse consisting of five iambic feet, e.g.

˘　/　˘　/　˘　　/　˘　/　˘　/
"Will stand a tip-toe when this day is nam'd"

image	the picture created in your mind by the poet's words
imagery	the use of images in poems
irregular	a rhythm which does not repeat similar patterns
lyric	a short, rhythmical poem; words to songs
masculine rhyme	rhyme in which one syllable only rhymes, e.g. "that man . . . his van"
metaphor	phrase comparing one thing with another by implying they are the same in a particular way, e.g. "the Moon danced across the sky" (note: metaphor does not use "as" or "like")
metre	the rhythmical pattern of a poem
monosyllable	word of one syllable
onomatopoeia	the use of words which sound like whatever they describe, e.g. "fizz", "splash"
quatrain	poetry verse with four lines
regular	a rhythm which repeats similar patterns
rhyme scheme	the pattern made by all the rhyming words in a poem
simile	phrase comparing one thing with another, e.g. "as white as snow", "like a red balloon"
single rhyme	(see masculine rhyme)
stress	the emphasis on that part of a word which is spoken loudest, e.g. the syllable "le" in "lemon"
syllable	the unit of rhythm in a word
thesaurus	a book in which words of similar meaning are found

SOURCES AND ACKNOWLEDGEMENTS

Permission to include certain poems has, it is believed, been made successfully. The form of acknowledgement, too, is thought to be in accordance with desire or stipulation. If, in any instance, neither the necessary permission has been sought nor the agreed credit made, sincere apology is offered for the omission or for any failure to meet specific requirements.

Anonymous:
Weathercock riddle from *The Earliest English Poems*, trans. Michael Alexander (Penguin Classics) 'A Spell to Destroy Life' and other charms from *The Puffin Book of Magic Verse*, ed. Charles Causley (Penguin)

Elizabeth Bishop:
'The Fish' from *Elizabeth Bishop: The Complete Poems, 1927–1979* © 1940, 1978. © 1978, 1983 by Alice Helen Methfessel. (Reprinted by Permission of Farrar, Straus and Giroux, Inc.)

Robert Browning:
lines from 'How They Brought the Good News from Ghent to Aix' from *The Poems of Robert Browning* (Oxford University Press)

Johnny Byrne:
'Siege' from *Children of Albion*, ed. Michael Horowitz (Penguin)

Lewis Carroll (Charles Lutwidge Dodgson):
'Jabberwocky' from *The New Oxford Book of English Verse*, ed. Helen Gardner (Oxford University Press)

Charles Causley:
'Timothy Winters' from *Collected Poems* (Macmillan)

G.K. Chesterton:
'The Donkey' and 'Lepanto' from *Collected Poems* (Methuen)

Tony Connor:
'Elegy for Alfred Hubbard' from *New and Selected Poems* (Anvil Press Poetry, 1982)

e.e. cummings:
'FOUR III' from *Complete Poems* (published by Graftor Books a division of The Harper Collins Publishing Group).

W.H. Davies:
'The Black Cloud' from *Complete Poems* (Jonathan Cape and the executors of the W.H. Davies estate)

Walter De La Mare:
'Alas, Alack!' from *Collected Rhymes and Verses* (Faber and Faber. Reproduced by kind permission of The Literary Trustees of Walter de la Mare and The Society of Authors as their representative.)

T.S. Eliot:
lines from *Murder in the Cathedral* (Reproduced by kind permission of Faber & Faber Ltd.)

Ian Hamilton Finlay:
'Acrobats' from *C'mon Everybody*, ed. Pete Morgan (Transworld Publishers) (Corgi)

H.G. Henderson (trans.):
'Bright the Full Moon' from *An Introduction to Haiku* (used by permission of Doubleday; a division of Bantam, Doubleday, Dell Publishing Group Inc.)

George Herbert:
'Easter Wings' from *The Metaphysical Poets*, ed. Helen Gardner (Penguin)

Ted Hipple:
'The Traditional Grammarian as Poet'

David Holbrook:
'The Happiest Places' from *The Quarry* (Musical setting by John Joubert, by permission of Novello & company Ltd.)

V.C. Horwell:
'In Memoriam: Alf Butterworth' quoted in *Telescopes*, ed. Eric Williams (Edward Arnold)

T.E. Hulme:
  'Autumn' from *Speculations* (Routledge & Kegan Paul)

James Joyce:
  'Goldenhair'

D.H. Lawrence:
  lines from 'Snake' from *The Complete Poems of D.H. Lawrence* (Lawrence Pollinger Ltd. and the estate of Mrs. Frieda Lawrence Ravagli)

Winifred M. Letts:
  'Tim the Irish Terrier' from *The Golden Anthology* (Blackie & Son Ltd)

H.W. Longfellow:
  lines from 'The Song of Hiawatha' (MacMillan Inc, New York)

Hugh MacDiarmid:
  lines from 'Perfect', quoted in *The Rattle Bag*, ed. Seamus Heaney and Ted Hughes (reproduced by permission of Martin O'Brian & O'Keefe Ltd. and the executor Michael Grieve)

Roger McGough:
  'Watchwords' from *Watchwords* (Jonathan Cape)

Herman Melville:
  lines from *Moby Dick*

Spike Milligan:
  'Ye Tortures' from *The Pot-Boiler* (Tandem Books)

A.A. Milne:
  lines from 'Bad Sir Brian Botany' from *When We Were Very Young* (Methuen)

Edwin Morgan:
  'The Loch Ness Monster's Song' from *From Glasgow to Saturn* and 'Spacepoem 3: Off Course' from *Poems of Thirty Years* (Carcanet Press Ltd)

Christian Morgenstern:
  'Night Song of the Fish'

Ogden Nash:
'Tableau at Twilight' Reprinted by permission of Curtis Brown Ltd. © 1942 by Ogden Nash)

Wilfred Owen:
'lines from 'From My Diary, July 1914' from *The Poems of Wilfred Owen* (Hogarth Press)

Sylvia Plath:
'Mirror' from *Collected Poems* (Faber and Faber) © Ted Hughes 1971, and 1981 and by permission of Olwyn Hughes)

Christina Rossetti:
'Ferryman'

P.B. Shelley:
'The Cloud' from *Poems by Percy Bysshe Shelley* (Unwin Hyman)

Jonathan Swift:
'A Gentle Echo on Woman' quoted in *Rhyme and Reason*, ed. Raymond O'Malley and Denys Thompson, (Hart-Davis Educational)

A.C. Swinburne:
lines from 'Atalanta in Calydon' from *Poems and Ballads* (Chatto & Windus)

Alfred Lord Tennyson:
lines from 'In Memoriam', 'Charge of the Light Brigade', 'The Eagle' and 'Sweet and Low' from *The Works of Alfred Lord Tennyson* (Macmillan)

Dylan Thomas:
lines from *Under Milk Wood* (J.M. Dent and Sons) and lines from *Collected Poems* quoted in *Dylan Thomas*, ed. C.B. Cox (Prentice-Hall, New Jersey)

R.S. Thomas:
'Death of a Peasant' © L.S. Thomas, 1972)

William Carlos Williams:
'This Is Just To Say'

INDEX